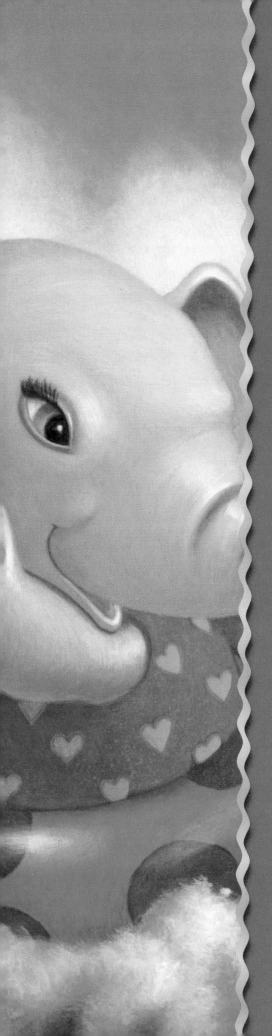

Scott Foresman
Reading

Let's Learn Together

About the Cover Artist
Maryjane Begin and her family live in Providence, Rhode Island, where she teaches college
students when she is not working on her own art. Many of her illustrations—even of imaginary
places—show how things in Providence look.

ISBN 0-673-62155-3

5 6 7 8 9 10-VH-06 05 04 03 02 01 00

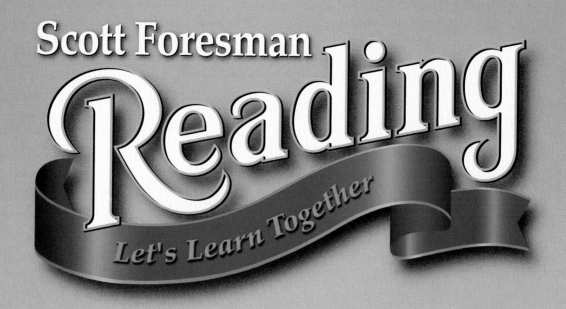

Scott Foresman Reading
Let's Learn Together

Program Authors

Peter Afflerbach

James Beers

Camille Blachowicz

Candy Dawson Boyd

Deborah Diffily

Dolores Gaunty-Porter

Violet Harris

Donald Leu

Susan McClanahan

Dianne Monson

Bertha Pérez

Sam Sebesta

Karen Kring Wixson

Scott Foresman

Editorial Offices: Glenview, Illinois • New York, New York
Sales Offices: Reading, Massachusetts • Duluth, Georgia • Glenview, Illinois
Carrollton, Texas • Menlo Park, California

Contents

Let's Learn Together

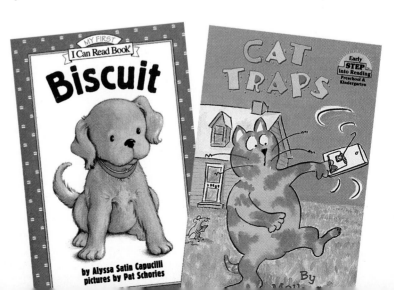

6

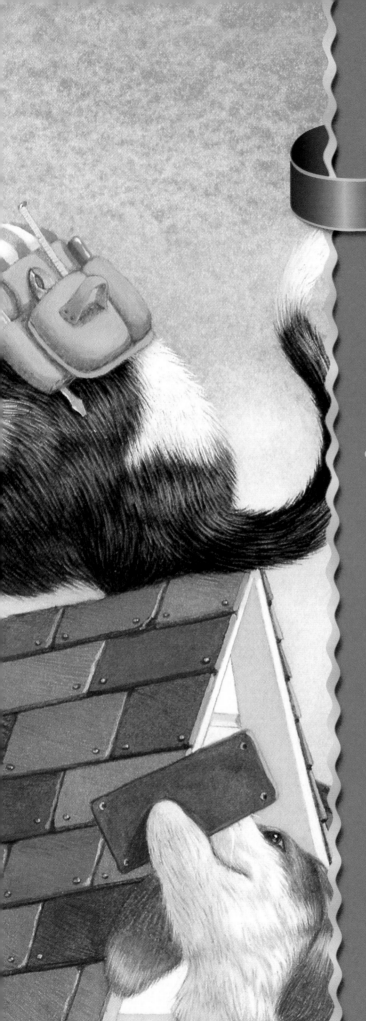

Let's Learn Together

What can we learn when we all work together?

The Big Mess

by B. G. Hennessy

illustrated by Christine Davenier

"Who made this mess?" said Tess.

"Can you help guess?" said Ben.

A mess in the hall.
A mess on the wall.

A mess on the floor.
A mess on the door.

So, was it the dog?
Was it the cat?

No, guess again.
It was baby Matt!

Now you see who
made the mess.

But who cleaned it up?
Can you guess?

The Little Red Hen

by Patricia and Fredrick McKissack

illustrated by John Sandford

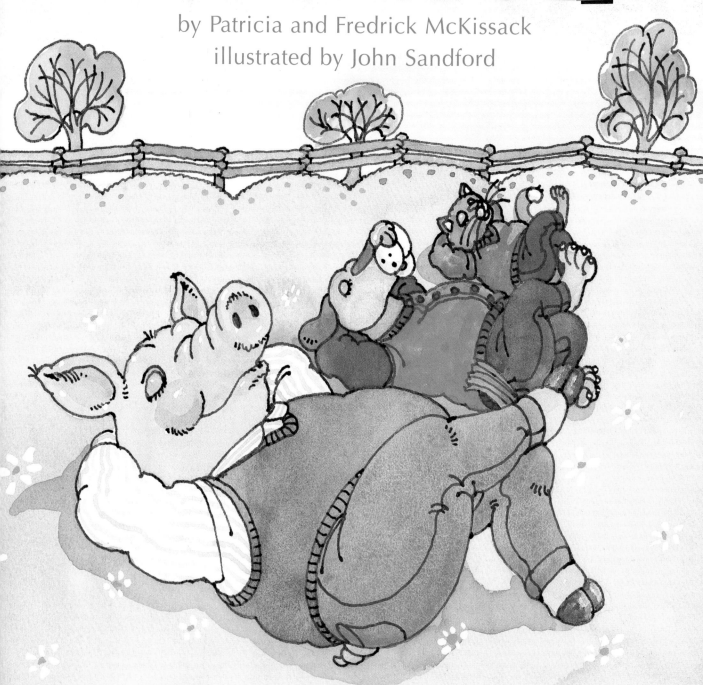

"Who will help me?" said
the Little Red Hen.

"Who me?"

"Why me?"

"Oh, no. Not me."

So the Little Red Hen
did it by herself.

"Who will help me?" said
the Little Red Hen.

So the Little Red Hen
did it by herself.

"No. I cannot."

"No. No. I cannot."

"No. No. No. I cannot."

So the Little Red Hen
did it by herself.

"Who will help me?" said
the Little Red Hen.

"Not now."

"No. No. Not now."

"Not now. Not now."

So the Little Red Hen
did it by herself.

"Who will help me?" said
the Little Red Hen.

"I will, next time."

"Yes. Next time."

"Yes. Yes. Next time."

So the Little Red Hen
did it by herself.

"Who will help me now?"
said the Little Red Hen.

"I cannot help."

"I cannot help."

"I cannot help."

So the Little Red Hen
did it by herself.

"Who will help me?" said
the Little Red Hen.

"I will!"

"Yes. I will too."

"I want to help too."

But the Little Red Hen said,
"No. No. No. You did not help me.
I will eat by myself."

About the Authors

Patricia and Fredrick McKissack met when they were teenagers. They both loved books. After they got married, they wrote books together.

The McKissacks like growing things in a garden just as the Little Red Hen does.

Let's Talk

The Little Red Hen asked for help.
She did not get any.
What would you do if
this happened to you?

Be a Helper

1. Pick one.

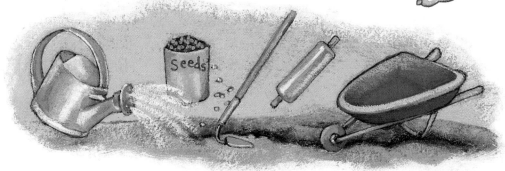

2. Tell how you would help the
Little Red Hen.

Who Can Help?

A **noun** is a word that names a person, place, animal, or thing.

The **girl** wipes the **dishes**.
The **cat** is in the **hall**.

Talk

Look at the picture.
Name the people, places,
animals, and things.
Then use the nouns
in sentences.

Write

Write about the story
The Little Red Hen.
What nouns will
you use?

Yes, We Want Some Too!

by Susan McCloskey

illustrated by Rosario Valderrama

The ten gray gulls are hungry.

They want some clams.

Mmm, good!

Yes, we want some too, please.

The black crows are hungry.

They want some fish.

Mmm, good!

Yes, we want some too, please.

The red hens are hungry.

They want some corn.

Mmm, good!

Yes, we want some too, please.

The green frogs are hungry.

They want some flies.

Ick! No flies for us!

Cat Traps

by Molly Coxe

Cat wants a snack.

Cat sets a trap.

Cat gets a bug.

Ugh!

Cat wants a snack.
Cat sets a trap.

Cat gets a pig.

Too big!

Cat wants a snack.

Cat sets a trap.

Cat gets a fish.
Swish!

Cat wants
a snack.
Cat sets
a trap.

Cat gets
a frog?

No, a dog!

Cat wants a snack.
Cat sets a trap.
Cat gets a duck.

Bad luck!

Cat wants a snack.

Cat sets a trap.

Cat gets—
a cat!

Drat.

Cat wants a snack.
Cat sets a trap.

Cat gets some chow.

Meow!

About the Author

Molly Coxe uses part of her garage as her studio. She works there while her children are in school. Her family has two cats, a dog, and a rabbit. One of their cats looks like the cat in *Cat Traps*.

Let's Talk

Pretend you are an animal that Cat trapped. What would you say to Cat?

Make a Snack Poster

Cat food is a good snack for a cat.
What is a good snack for you?
Show your snack on a poster.

What you need:

paper plate

pencils, crayons, and markers

glue

poster

What you do:

1. Draw your snack on the plate.

2. Glue your plate on a poster.

Dog or Dogs?

Sometimes **-s** is added to the end of a noun. An **-s** makes a noun mean more than one.

dog

dogs

Talk

Tell about the picture. What nouns will you use? Do they mean more than one?

Write

List the animals in *Cat Traps.* Write each animal name to mean more than one.

My Buddy, Stan

by Deborah Eaton

illustrated by Shelly Hehenberger

I am Pug.

This is my buddy, Stan.

Stan is lots of fun.

I let Stan pat me.
I let him brush me.
He likes it!

I let Stan run with me.
I let him jump with me.
He likes it!

I let Stan play with me.
I let him tug at a stick.
He likes it!

I let Stan feed me too.
That snack smells good.
Yum! More, please.

Time to go to sleep.

But Stan wants to hug me.

I can tell.

I like it!
So I let him.
What a good hug!

Good boy, Stan.
Good boy!

Biscuit

by Alyssa Satin Capucilli
illustrated by Pat Schories

This is Biscuit.

Biscuit is small.

Biscuit is yellow.

Time for bed, Biscuit!

Woof, woof!

Biscuit wants to play.

Time for bed, Biscuit!

Woof, woof!

Biscuit wants a snack.

Time for bed, Biscuit!

Woof, woof!

Biscuit wants a drink.

Time for bed, Biscuit!

Woof, woof!

Biscuit wants to hear a story.

Time for bed, Biscuit!

Woof, woof!

Biscuit wants his blanket.

Time for bed, Biscuit!

Woof, woof!

Biscuit wants his doll.

Time for bed, Biscuit!

Woof, woof!

Biscuit wants a hug.

Time for bed, Biscuit!

Woof, woof!

Biscuit wants a kiss.

Time for bed, Biscuit!
Woof, woof!
Biscuit wants a light on.

Woof!

Biscuit wants to be tucked in.

Woof!

Biscuit wants one more kiss.

Woof!

Biscuit wants one more hug.

Woof!

Biscuit wants to curl up.

Sleepy puppy.
Good night, Biscuit.

About the Author and the Illustrator

Alyssa Satin Capucilli lives with her husband and two children. She has written other books about Biscuit. One is called *Biscuit Finds a Friend.*

Author

Pat Schories has a dog named Spike. She used Spike as the model for Biscuit. Ms. Schories has illustrated other books for children.

Illustrator

Puppy

by Lee Bennett Hopkins

We bought our puppy
   A brand new bed
But he likes sleeping
   On mine instead.

I'm glad he does
   'Cause I'd miss his cold nose

Waking me up,
   Tickling my toes.

Let's Talk

How is your bedtime
like Biscuit's bedtime?
How is it different?

Puppy Puppets

What you need:

paper bags

crayons or markers

art supplies

What you do:

Make a puppy face.

Cut out puppy ears.

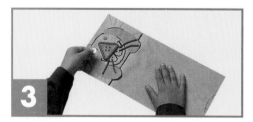

Put ears on the puppy.
Add more things.

4 Act out the story.

People and Pets

People and pets have **special names**.

Special names begin with capital letters.

Patty plays with **Jet**.

Jim feeds **Ed** and **Bob**.

Talk

What are the special names of people in your family?
Tell the special names of pets you know.

Write

Write about a pet. Give the pet a special name.

Trucks

by Gail Saunders-Smith

Trucks carry logs.

Trucks haul garbage.

Trucks hold milk.

Trucks mix cement.

Trucks dump rocks.

Trucks plow snow.

Trucks tow cars.

Trucks bring mail.

Communities

by Gail Saunders-Smith

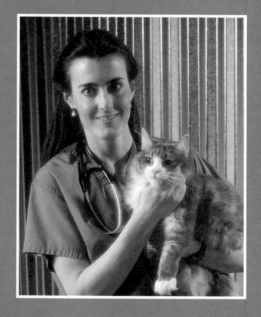

Police officers help us stay safe.

Doctors help us
stay healthy.

Teachers help
us learn.

Coaches help
us play.

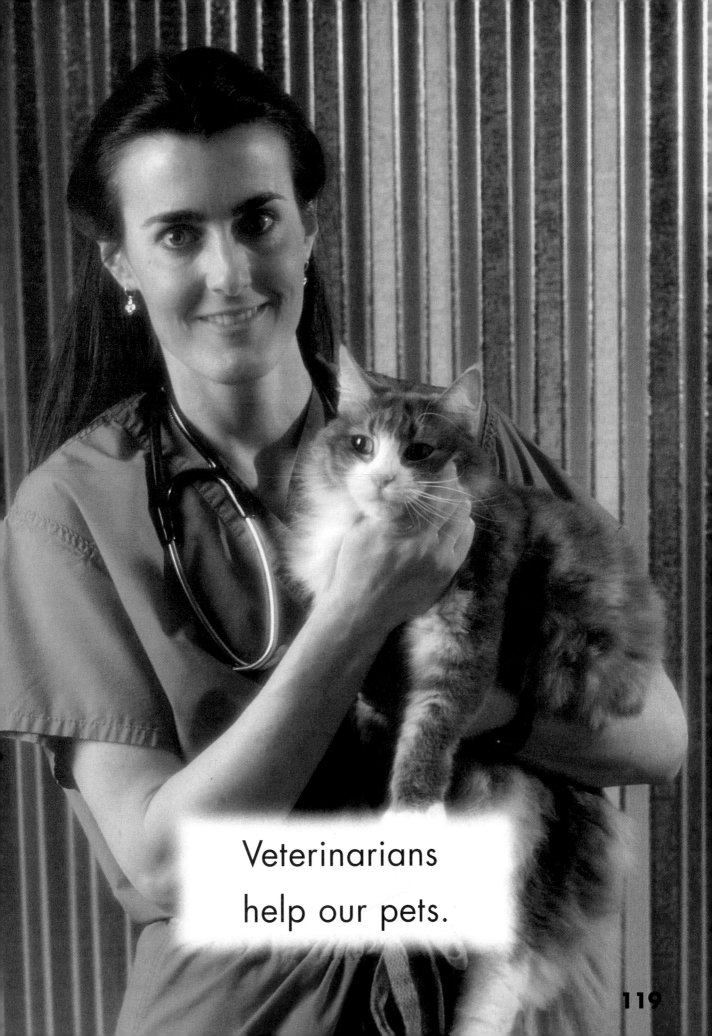

Veterinarians
help our pets.

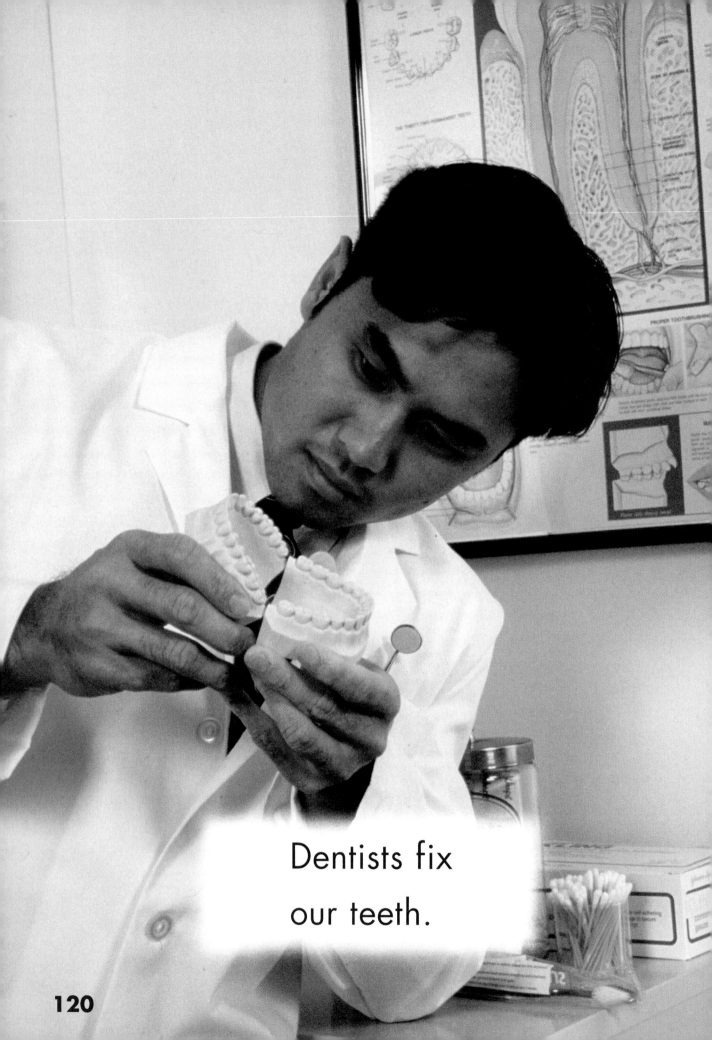

Dentists fix
our teeth.

Fire fighters save
our homes.

Mail carriers
bring our mail.

Construction workers build our roads.

Words to Know

coach—a person who trains a sports team

construction worker—a person who builds buildings or roads

dentist—a person who is trained to examine and fix teeth

doctor—a person who is trained to help people stay healthy

fire fighter—a person who is trained to put out fires

mail carrier—a person who delivers or picks up mail

police officer—a person who is trained to make sure people obey the law

teacher—a person who is trained to show others how to do something

veterinarian—a person who is trained to treat sick and injured animals

About the Author

Gail Saunders-Smith
has written many nonfiction
books for young readers.
You know that she wrote
about trucks and communities.
She has also written about
nature and animals.

Let's Talk

You read about workers.
Which workers have helped
you the most?
Tell how the workers helped.

Be a Worker

Choose your job.
Tell what you do.
Tell why your job
is important.

My Mom, the Doctor

A **title** can come before
the name of the person.
A title begins with a
capital letter.
Some titles end with a **.** .

My mother is **Dr.** Meg Waters.
My father is **Mr.** Cal Waters.

Mr. Matt Dunn
Dr. Ned Horn
Mrs. Kim Sing
Mayor Jan Zampa
Ms. Tessa Link
Mr. John Block
Mrs. Pat O'Shea

Talk

What titles are on
the list?
What does the title tell
you about the person?

Write

Who works in your school?
Make a list of people.
Write titles with their
names.

Fox and Bear

by David McPhail

Fox ran to Bear's house.

Fox ran up.

Fox ran down.

Fox ran too fast.

Fox ran past the house.

Bear ran after Fox.

"Look," said Bear.

"Come back."

Fox came back.

He sat down for a chat.

"You can run fast," said Bear.

"Yes, I know," said Fox.

"I am glad you saw me!"
said Fox.

"I am glad too," said Bear.

Fox and Bear
Look at the Moon
by David McPhail

Fox and Bear sat.

"Look," said Bear.

"Look at the moon."

"It looks fat," said Fox.

"Yes, I know," said Bear.

"It does look fat."

Fox had a nap.

Bear sat and sat.

She looked at the moon.

The moon moved.

Bear gave Fox a tap.

Tap, tap.

"Look, Fox," said Bear.

"The moon is gone!"

Fox sat up.

"Where did it go?" asked Fox.

"Maybe it fell," said Bear.

Fox looked down.

There was the moon.

"I can get it out," said Fox.

"I can jump in!"

"Look," said Bear.

"The moon came back!"

"I got it out," said Fox.

"Yes, you did," said Bear.

Bear gave Fox a pat.

A big pat on the back.

Pat. Pat.

About the Author and Illustrator

David McPhail says that as a child he drew "anywhere, anytime, and on anything!" His love of drawing sometimes got him into trouble. He learned not to draw on walls!

Many of Mr. McPhail's books have animals in them. He really enjoys drawing bears.

Let's Talk

Fox said the moon looks fat.
Does the moon always
look the same to you?
Why or why not?

Write a Story

Think about what Fox
and Bear do next.

1. Write about what
   they do next.
2. Draw a picture to
   go with your story.

Fox and Bear swim in the water.

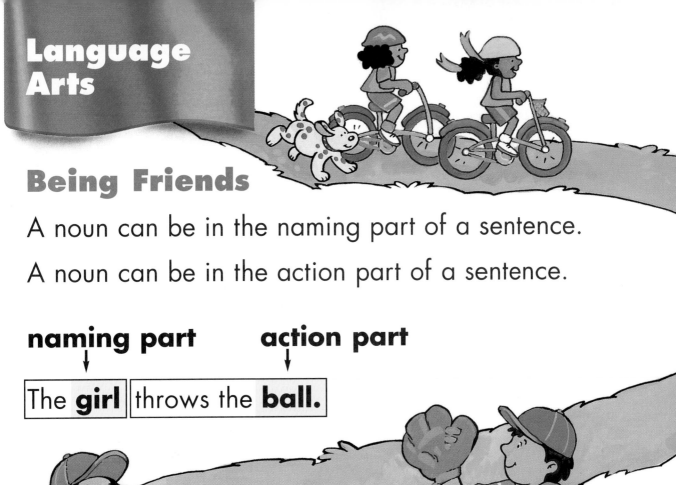

Being Friends

A noun can be in the naming part of a sentence.

A noun can be in the action part of a sentence.

naming part   **action part**

The **girl** | throws the **ball.**

Talk

Tell about a friend.
What is special about your friend?
What does your friend like to do?

Write

Write about a friend.
Tell what your friend is like.

151

I Can Read

by Judy Nayer

illustrated by Jennifer Beck Harris

I can read.

It's fun to do!

Please come with me.

I'll read to you!

I'll read the list

that's on this pad.

milk
nuts
six plums
ham
eggs
jam

I'll read the word
that's on my dad.

I'll read the words
there on the grass.

I'll walk and say

the words I pass.

Next come with me.

I know just where.

Yes! I see them!

More words are there!

The Den

lamps
rugs
beds
cribs

Hat Hut

hats
caps
wigs

Now I'll say
the words again.
Please read with me.
I'll bet you can!

Lilly Reads

by Laurie
Krasny Brown

illustrated by
Marc Brown

"Lilly," said Mrs. Woo,
"please read the next
page out loud.
Page six."

Lilly looked at page six.

She read,

"Long, long ago
in a far-off land,
there lived an elf
who was a bit of a . . ."

Lilly stopped.

"Very good, Lilly," said Mrs. Woo.
"Please go on."

Lilly looked at page six.
"I can't go on!" she said.
"I can't read the next word. It's too—"

"I can! I can!" Willy called out.

"But, Willy," said Mrs. Woo.

"It's Lilly's turn.

   You can read this word, Lilly,"

 she said.

"You can sound it out."

"It's too hard!" said Lilly.

Willy called out again,
"I can sound it out!
I can sound out this word."

"But, Willy, it's still Lilly's turn,"
said Mrs. Woo.
"Lilly, just try!"

So Lilly said the sounds out loud,
"P

   E."

"It's a short e, as in e*lf*," said Mrs. Woo.
"S

   T."

"Now say them again,"
said Mrs. Woo.

Lilly said them again.
"P-e-s-t."
And again.
She said them faster.
And faster.

All of a sudden Lilly stopped
and looked at page six.
Then she read right out loud,
"Long, long ago
in a far-off land,
there lived an elf
who was a bit of a . . .
pest!"

"Yes!" said Mrs. Woo.
"Good work, Lilly!"

"And, Willy," said Lilly,
"that goes for you too.
You are a bit of a pest!"

Then Lilly read
and read
and read.

About the Author

Laurie Krasny Brown enjoys writing stories that young readers can read on their own.

Her husband, Marc Brown, drew the pictures for "Lilly Reads." He often does the drawings for her stories.

You can read more about Lilly and her brother, Rex. Ms. Brown has written several books about them.

Books Books Books

by Kay Winters

I LOVE TO READ!
Say those words.
Go those places.
See those sights.
Think those thoughts.
Meet those kids
who live in books,
waiting for me
to find them.

Let's Talk

Pretend that you helped Lilly read.
What else could you tell her to
do that would help her read?

Book Talk

What book would you
tell Lilly to read?
Tell what she would
like about it.

172

Special Times

The names of days, months, and holidays begin with capital letters.

February

Sunday	Monday	Tuesday	Wednesday	Thursday	Friday	Saturday
1	2 Groundhog Day	3	4	5	6	7
8	9	10	11	12	13	14 Valentine's Day
15	16 Presidents' Day	17	18	19	20	21

Talk

Look at the calendar. What words begin with capital letters?

Write

Write about a holiday. What month is it in? What day is it on? Tell why it is special.

173

What We Do

feed

carry

hold

read

sleep

haul

tow

build

bring

chat

jump

hear

clean

175

Tested Word List

The Big Mess
The Little Red Hen

help
now
said
so
who

**Yes, We Want
Some Too!**
Cat Traps

for
good
some
too
want

My Buddy, Stan
Biscuit

jump
more
sleep
time
with

Trucks
Communities

bring
carry
hold
our
us

Fox and Bear
**Fox and Bear
Look at the Moon**

came
know
out
she
there

I Can Read
Lilly Reads

again
please
read
say
word

Acknowledgments

Text

Page 18: *The Little Red Hen* by Patricia and Fredrick McKissack, pp. 3–28 & 30. Copyright © 1985 by Regensteiner Publishing Enterprises, Inc. Reprinted by permission of Grolier Publishing Company.
Page 46: *Cat Traps* by Molly Coxe, pp. 4–32. Copyright © 1996 by Molly Coxe. Reprinted by permission of Random House, Inc.
Page 82: *Biscuit* by Alyssa Satin Capucilli, pictures by Pat Schories, pp. 6–26. Text copyright © 1996 by Alyssa Satin Capucilli. Illustrations copyright © 1996 by Pat Schories. Reprinted by permission of HarperCollins Publishers, Inc.
Page 103: "Puppy" from *Good Rhymes, Good Times* by Lee Bennett Hopkins, pg. 9. Copyright © 1974, 1995 by Lee Bennett Hopkins. Published by HarperCollins Publishers, Inc. Reprinted by permission of Curtis Brown, Ltd.
Page 106: *Trucks* by Gail Saunders-Smith, pp. 5, 7, 9, 11, 13, 15, 17, 19, & 21–22. Copyright © 1998 by Pebble Books, an imprint of Capstone Press. Reprinted by permission of Capstone Press.
Page 114: *Communities* by Gail Saunders-Smith, pp. 5, 7, 9, 11, 13, 15, 17, 19, & 21–22. Copyright © 1998 by Pebble Books, an imprint of Capstone Press. Reprinted by permission of Capstone Press.
Pages 128, 136: © David McPhail
Page 160: "Lilly Reads" from *Rex and Lilly Schooltime* by Laurie Krasny Brown, pictures by Marc Brown, pp. 23–32. Copyright © 1997 by Laurene Krasny Brown and Marc Brown. Reprinted by permission of Little, Brown and Company.

Page 171: "Books Books Books" from *Did You See What I Saw?* by Kay Winters, illustrated by Martha Weston. Text copyright © 1996 by Kay Winters. Illustrations copyright © 1996 by Martha Weston. Reprinted by permission of Viking Penguin, a division of Penguin Putnam, Inc.

Artists

Maryjane Begin, cover, 8–9
Iskra Johnson, (calligraphy) 9
Christine Davenier, 10–17
John Sandford, 18–35
Mary N. DePalma, 36–37
Rosario Valderrama, 38–45
Molly Coxe, 46–71
Randy Chewning, 72–73
Shelly Hehenberger, 74–81
Pat Schories, 82–101
Anthony Carnabuci, 104–105
Eileen Mueller-Neill, 127
David McPhail, 128–149
Anastasia Mitchell, 150–151
Jennifer Harris, 152–159
Marc Brown, 160–169
Martha Weston, 171
Mike Dammer, 172–173
Kathy McCord, 174–175

Photographs

Page 6 Richard Hutchings for Scott Foresman
Page 35 Courtesy the McKissacks
Page 71 Courtesy Molly Coxe

Page 73 PhotoDisc, Inc.
Page 102 (T) Courtesy Scholastic; (B) Courtesy Pat Schories
Page 103 Ron Kimball
Page 106 Brian Atkinson/Valan Photos
Page 107 H. H. Thomas/Unicorn Stock Photos
Page 108 David R. Frazier/David R. Frazier Photolibrary
Page 109 Jeff Greenberg/Unicorn Stock Photos
Page 110 J. A. Wilkinson/Valan Photos
Page 111 Michael J. Johnson/Valan Photos
Page 112 Florent Flipper/Unicorn Stock Photos
Page 113 Aneal Vohra/Unicorn Stock Photos
Page 114 (TL) Arthur Tilley/FPG International Corp.; (TR) Tom Tracy/FPG International Corp.; (BL) James Blank/FPG International Corp.; (BR) Elizabeth Simpson/FPG International Corp.
Page 115 Michael Nelson/FPG International Corp.
Page 116 Mike Malyszko/FPG International Corp.
Page 117 Arthur Tilley/FPG International Corp.
Page 118 Andrew Farquhar/Valan Photos
Page 119 Elizabeth Simpson/FPG International Corp.
Page 120 Tom McCarthy/Unicorn Stock Photos
Page 121 Tom Tracy/FPG International Corp.
Page 122 James Blank/FPG International Corp.
Page 123 Bill Losh/FPG International Corp.
Page 125 (CC) Courtesy Gail Saunders-Smith; (TL, TR, TLC, CL, BR) PhotoDisc, Inc.; (TRC) Shock/Stock Imagery, Inc.; (CR) J. A. Wilkinson/Valan Photos; (BL) Tony Joyce/Valan Photos
Page 149 Richard Hutchings for Scott Foresman
Page 170 Courtesy Little, Brown and Company